Ripley's Believe It or Not!

Developed and produced by Ripley Publishing Ltd

This edition published and distributed by:

Mason Crest
450 Parkway Drive, Suite D, Broomall, PA 19008
www.masoncrest.com

Printed and bound in the United States of America

First printing
9 8 7 6 5 4 3 2 1

Ripley's Believe It or Not!
Amazing People
ISBN: 978-1-4222-2770-1 (hardback)
ISBN: 978-1-4222-2787-9 (paperback)
ISBN: 978-1-4222-9031-6 (e-book)
Ripley's Believe It or Not!—Complete 8 Title Series
ISBN: 978-1-4222-2769-5

Cataloging-in-Publication Data on file with the Library of Congress

PUBLISHER'S NOTE
While every effort has been made to verify the accuracy of the entries in this book, the
Publisher's cannot be held responsible for any errors contained in the work. They would
be glad to receive any information from readers.

WARNING
Some of the stunts and activities in this book are undertaken by experts and should not
be attempted by anyone without adequate training and supervision.

Ripley's Believe It or Not!

Enter If You Dare

AMAZING PEOPLE

www.MasonCrest.com

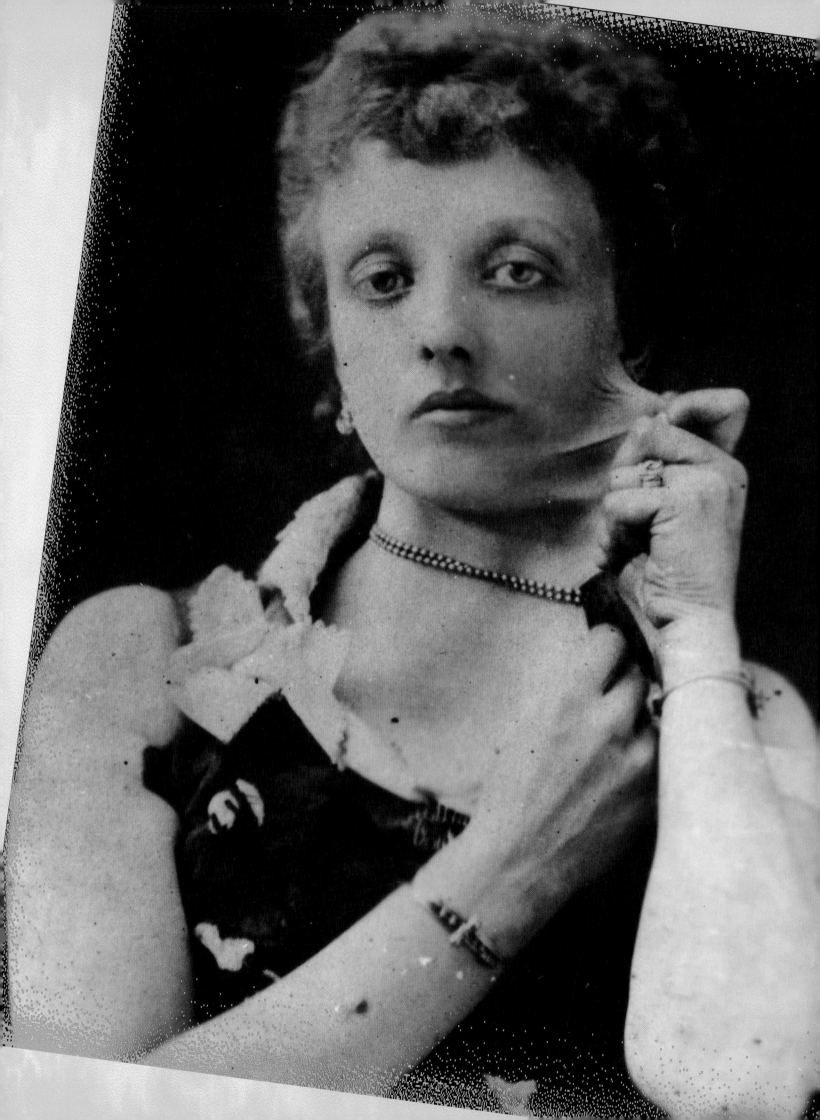

AMAZING PEOPLE

Life's curiosities. Be amazed at
some of the most unbelievable
body stories. Discover the man with
over 240 body piercings, the girl with
elastic skin, and the 16-year-old teenager
who is only 23½ in (60 cm) tall.

Etta Lake became famous for the very elastic
skin on her cheeks and neck...

Tiny Teen

SIXTEEN-YEAR-OLD JYOTI AMGE FROM NAGPUR, INDIA, IS ONE OF THE SMALLEST TEENAGERS IN THE WORLD, STANDING ONLY 23.5 IN (60 CM) TALL AND WEIGHING A LITTLE OVER 11 LB (5 KG). DESPITE WEIGHING ONLY 9 LB (4 KG) MORE THAN SHE DID WHEN SHE WAS BORN, JYOTI SAYS SHE IS NO DIFFERENT FROM OTHER PEOPLE. SHE IS PROUD TO BE SMALLER, AND ENJOYS ALL THE EXTRA ATTENTION SHE RECEIVES.

JYOTI TRAVELS TO THE LOCAL SCHOOL ON HER BROTHER'S MOTORBIKE ALONG WITH HER SISTERS WHERE SHE MIXES WITH ALL HER SCHOOL FRIENDS.

IN THE CLASSROOM SHE HAS A CUSTOM-MADE DESK NEXT TO THE OTHER PUPILS. SHE HAS A LARGE COLLECTION OF DRESSES LIKE ANY TEENAGER, AND DREAMS OF BECOMING AN ACTRESS—SHE HAS ALREADY STARRED IN A VIDEO WITH INDIAN POP STAR MIKA SINGH.

MONSTER ARMS

THE IRONICALLY NAMED TINY IRON, FROM LONDON, ENGLAND, HAS ENORMOUS BICEPS THAT MEASURE AN INCREDIBLE 24 IN (61 CM) IN CIRCUMFERENCE—THAT'S BIGGER THAN MOST PEOPLE'S THIGHS—AND CAN SMASH AN EGG WHEN FLEXED! IN THE PAST, TINY PUT HIS MASSIVE ARMS TO USE AS A BODYGUARD, BUT HE IS NOW AN ACTOR AND WRESTLER. IN ORDER TO FUEL HIS 280-LB (127-KG) FRAME, HE EATS A HEAVYWEIGHT DIET OF HIGH-PROTEIN CHICKEN BREASTS FOR BREAKFAST, LUNCH, AND DINNER.

Larger than life

In October 2011, Tiny Iron met Khagendra Thapa Magar from Nepal, one of the world's smallest men, measuring just 22 in (56 cm) in height, at the Ripley's Believe it or Not! Museum in Piccadilly Circus, London. The diameter of Tiny Iron's biceps is greater than the height of Khagendra's body! They met to promote the Ripley's Believe it or Not! book *Enter If You Dare!*

℞ METEORITE HIT

In June 2009, 14-year-old Gerrit Blank survived after being hit by a meteorite that crashed to Earth in Essen, Germany, at 30,000 mph (48,000 km/h). The red-hot piece of rock about the size of a pea appeared as a ball of light before bouncing off his hand and causing a 1-ft-wide (30-cm) crater in the ground. The 100 million-to-one strike knocked him off his feet and left him with a 3-in (7.6-cm) scar on his hand. The noise that followed the flash of light was so loud that his ears were ringing for hours afterward.

℞ HORSE LEGS

Seattle, Washington State, designer Kim Graham has devised the ultimate accessory for people who want to look taller and more elegant—horse leg extensions. Her Digitigrade Leg Extensions, which are shaped like a horse's leg, are made of steel, cable, foam, and rigid plastic and add 14 in (35 cm) of height to the wearer. She says it takes only 15 minutes to learn to walk in them, although the wearer should avoid stairs. The standard legs cost $750—with another $200 for spring-loaded hooves to put an extra bounce in your step.

℞ SOLITARY TREE

On vacation in Tenerife, 66-year-old grandmother Maureen Evason from Plymouth, England, was saved from a fatal fall off a 150-ft-high (45-m) volcanic ridge when her head became wedged in the only tree on the mountain. Her head was stuck for three hours between two branches, which provided a natural neck brace to immobilize her body and prevent spinal injuries.

℞ UNIQUE BONE

The hyoid bone, just above the larynx, anchors the muscles of the tongue and is the only bone in the human body that doesn't touch any other.

℞ VISION RESTORED

A 70-year-old man who had been "as blind as a bat" for his entire life suddenly acquired perfect vision after suffering a massive stroke. Retired architect Malcolm Darby from Leicestershire, England, had worn thick glasses since the age of two, but when he came to after surgery to clear the blood clot that had caused his stroke, he found that for the first time in his life he could see clearly without them.

℞ THREE GENERATIONS

In August 2009, three generations of the same family were born within 30 minutes of each other in the same hospital in Dublin, Ireland. Family matriarch Eileen McGuinness, 85, was blessed with her 69th grandchild, her 58th great-grandchild, and her first great-great-grandchild in startlingly quick succession. Amazingly, none of the three expectant mothers knew the others were in the hospital at the time they were each preparing to give birth.

℞ BAT BOY

A blind English boy has learned to "see" the world around him for the first time by using echolocation—the technique used by bats and dolphins. By clicking his tongue on the roof of his mouth, Lucas Murray from Dorset, England, can discover where and how big objects are depending on the echoes that bounce back. He uses the method to play basketball, determining which direction the hoop is in and how far away it is before making his shot.

SHARK ATTACK

After a great white shark bit a chunk out of 13-year-old Hannah Mighall's surfboard and dragged her under the water, the teenager's life was saved by her cousin and fellow surfer, Syb Munday, who swam out to her and began punching the shark on the head. The 16-ft-long (4.9-m) predator, which had attacked off Binalong Bay in Tasmania, Australia, let Hannah go and she survived with bites to her legs that required 200 stitches.

THOUGHT PROCESS

Paralyzed neuroscientist Scott Mackler relies on a computer system that translates thoughts into text, to enable him to continue his work at the University of Pennsylvania. He wears a special cap that picks up the electrical activity of his brain and allows him to select letters just by thinking about them. The computer then turns his sentences into speech.

SWALLOWED PIN

Doctors in China discovered the cause of an eight-year-old boy's constant coughs and colds—a rusty thumbtack stuck in his right lung. Xiao Ming of Mingguang, Anhui Province, had been suffering from the mystery ailments for a year.

STAYIN' ALIVE

A Massachusetts woman revived her husband from cardiac arrest by administering CPR to the beat of the Bee Gees' disco classic "Stayin' Alive." After he collapsed during a walk, she remembered a public service announcement by the American Heart Association. It advised people untrained in CPR to help heart attack victims by compressing their chest 100 times a minute and to use "Stayin' Alive," which has 103 beats a minute, as a handy guideline.

MEMORY MAN

Bob Petrella, a television producer in his fifties from Los Angeles, California, can remember almost everything he has done in life since the age of five. He can recall precise details of virtually all his birthdays, along with every New Year's Eve for the last 40 years, and all the conversations he has had on most days throughout the last 53 years. He has been diagnosed with the condition hyperthymestia (overdeveloped memory), which has been discovered in just four people around the world.

MIGHTY ATOM

In 2009, at three years of age, Liam Hoekstra from Grand Rapids, Michigan, could shift furniture, lift 5-lb (2.3-kg) weights, do sit-ups, and perform incredible gymnastic feats of strength. Although he is smaller than most children his age, he has a rare condition that causes his body to have very little fat and 40 percent more muscle mass. As he has a fast metabolism, he eats up to six meals a day.

PICKLED LEG

Song Weiguo of Jiangyan, China, has preserved his amputated leg in formaldehyde for more than 20 years to warn others of the perils of drunk driving. Having drunk a pint of strong liquor, he lost his left leg in a motorcycle crash in 1989 and now puts the severed limb on display every year on the anniversary of the accident.

Spooky Eyes

Hollywood special-effects artist Kevin Carter creates colored contact lenses, which can make the wearer look as if he or she has been possessed by demons or is an alien visitor from another planet. He spends up to two days hand-painting dye onto each lens with a fine brush, and his scary designs—which also include a shark's open jaws—can sell for up to $750 a pair.

Arm Lock

Justin Shaw, a professional drummer from Kentucky, takes pride in his exceptionally long arm hair. The longest hair measures a lengthy 5¾ in (14.6 cm), long enough to stretch around a large grapefruit. Justin has always liked the long blond arm tufts, and has never wanted to cut them short. However, since he moved to Miami, Florida, he has recorded a faster growth in his arm hairs—something he puts down to "getting a lot of vitamin D" in the sunshine—yet he still has no desire to cut them.

R NEVER WASHES

A man in India who fathered seven daughters has not washed for more than 35 years in an attempt to guarantee that his next child is a boy. Instead of bathing traditionally and brushing his teeth, 63-year-old Kailash Singh, from a village near Varanasi, has a "fire bath" every evening when he stands on one leg beside a bonfire and says prayers. Apparently a seer had once told him that if he did not take a normal bath, he would be blessed with a male child.

R KIDNEY STONE

In January 2009, doctors removed a kidney stone that was the size of a coconut from the body of Sandor Sarkadi in Debrecen, Hungary.

R SNOWDRIFT

Fifty-five-year-old Donna Molnar of Ancaster, Ontario, Canada, collapsed in a snowdrift in December 2008 and survived three days of sub-zero temperatures and blowing winds until she was rescued. She was eventually found buried in 2 ft (60 cm) of snow, with all but her face and neck covered.

R SPAT BULLET

After Richard Jamison of Bridgeton, New Jersey, was shot in the face in February 2009, he spat the bullet out of his mouth, then went looking for help.

R CHOPSTICK OP

A Chinese kung-fu master, who accidentally swallowed a chopstick during a training stunt, forgot that it was lodged in his stomach for 20 years until it suddenly started to cause him pain. Forty-year-old Wing Ma finally had the 7-in-long (18-cm) chopstick removed in 2009 during an operation in eastern Wuhan.

R FOOD FOR THOUGHT

Researchers in Quebec, Canada, have discovered that thinking too hard can make people fat. Blood tests on student volunteers showed that those who had recently taken an exam ate more because the brain workout sent their glucose and insulin levels haywire, making them hungrier.

R FACIAL TUMOR

Fifteen-year-old Lai Thi Dao of Vietnam underwent a 12-hour surgery in April 2008 to remove a tumor that accounted for one-third of her body weight. It started out as little more than a cyst on her tongue when she was three, but grew to weigh over 12 lb (5.4 kg) and consumed the lower half of her face.

R EXTRA DIGITS

Kamani Hubbard was born in San Francisco, California, in January 2009 with 24 fingers and toes. The 24 were made up of six digits on each of his hands and feet, and were perfectly formed and fully functioning.

R HAND SEVERED

Mr. Shi of Shenzen, China, lost his hand in 2009 when it was pulled off at the wrist during a beach tug-of-war contest. Doctors successfully reattached the severed hand in a five-hour operation.

R SELFLESS SURGEON

Italian surgeon Claudio Vitale finished a brain operation on a patient in March 2009 despite suffering a heart attack partway through the procedure. Dr. Vitale realized his patient would never recover if he halted the operation to seek treatment for himself, so he continued for another 30 minutes in the operating theatre at Cardarelli Hospital, Naples, until the patient was out of danger.

R ARM RECOVERED

After 11-year-old Devin Funck from Slidell, Louisiana, had his arm bitten off by a huge alligator in a lake near New Orleans in 2008, wildlife officials shot the reptile and recovered the arm largely intact from its stomach.

℞ IMPROVISED DRILL

Rob Carson, a doctor in Maryborough, Victoria, Australia, used a handyman's power drill to bore into a boy's skull and relieve potentially fatal bleeding on his brain. Nicholas Rossi had seriously injured his head falling off his bicycle, but the small hospital did not have neurological drills, so Dr. Carson sent for a household drill from the maintenance room and called a neurosurgeon in Melbourne to talk him through the complex procedure, which he had never previously attempted.

Patient Pinky

Sheng Wang, from Fujian, China, left one of his pinky fingernails to grow for 15 years, until it measured an amazing 18 in (46 cm) in length. In 1996, Wang decided to grow the nail for as long as he could to become a more peaceful person and test his patience. He has loved the change so much that he even turned down an offer of nearly $10,000 to remove the nail.

℞ SPECIAL BRANCH

John Nash, a rookie police officer from Rochdale, England, fell while pursuing a suspect, but didn't realize he had impaled his eye socket on the branch of a bush until after he caught and arrested the perpetrator. The 6-in (15-cm) piece of wood snapped off, but it had pierced his eyelid, smashed a cheekbone, forced itself under his eyeball, and had come to rest against his brain.

℞ HUMAN TREE

Surgeons operating on a man in Russia in 2009 discovered a tree growing inside his lungs. They think that 28-year-old Artyom Sidorkin had somehow inhaled a seed, which subsequently sprouted inside his lung. The 2-in-long (5-cm) spruce was touching his capillaries and causing him extreme chest pain.

℞ STRONG GIRL

Jacqueline Wickens from Elko, Nevada, deadlifted 308 lb (140 kg) in Anaheim, California, in December 2007—even though she was only 13 years old.

℞ HYPNOTIC DENTIST

In May 2008, Leslie Mason from Essex, England, underwent two hours of root canal work without anesthetic after being hypnotized by his friend John Ridlington. Despite having two upper right molars removed along with their roots, plus two roots from teeth that had been pulled in the 1980s, the patient reported feeling nothing more than "a little sting."

℞ EXTENDED LEAVE

Left unable to walk or talk by a road accident that nearly killed him, computer worker Karl McLennan of Aberdeen, Scotland, returned to his job in 2009 after 12 years of sick leave.

℞ TOO PASSIONATE

In December 2008, a man in Zhuhai, Guangdong, China, kissed his girlfriend so passionately that it popped her eardrum and she went deaf in that ear.

℞ HAIR DETERRENT

Farmers in Malaysia have been gathering sacks of human hair from barber shops to prevent wild boar from destroying their young oil palms. They spread the hair around the crops, and when a boar sniffs the hair, it thinks humans are present and runs off.

Supple Skin

The "girl with the elastic skin" pictured here was famous for the stretchy skin on her cheeks and neck. Etta Lake, who traveled with the King–Franklin Circus in 1889, could pull the skin an amazing 6 in (15 cm) from her cheek.

℞ BIG BABY

In September 2009, an Indonesian woman gave birth to a baby boy weighing a whopping 19.2 lb (8.7 kg). The baby, who is 24.4 in (62 cm) long, was born by cesarean section at a hospital in North Sumatra province.

℞ LUCKY STRIKE

When Nada Acimovich of Sljivovica, Serbia, was struck by lightning, she was saved by her rubber-soled shoes—and the electric jolt cured her deadly heart condition. Her condition, known as arrhythmia, is normally treated with mild electric shocks to reset the heart's rhythm.

℞ LONG STRAND

Brian Peterkin-Vertanesian of Washington, D.C., boasts a single red eyebrow hair that measures an incredible 6 3/8 in (16.2 cm) long. The hair, which he has named Wally, is long enough for him to chew on, although he usually keeps it tucked behind his left ear for safety.

Ripley's Revealed

Twisted ART

Contortionists defy physical boundaries by twisting their body into seemingly impossible, backbreaking positions. Fully grown adults can squeeze their entire body through an unstrung tennis racket that is 10 in (25 cm) in diameter or a toilet seat, or into a glass bottle that is just 2 ft (0.6 m) high. Or they tie their body into intricate knots with their legs wrapped around the back of their neck and touching each other.

The art of contortionism is depicted in ancient Roman, Egyptian, and Greek sculptures and has been featured in the Buddhist Tsam dance for centuries. In Mongolia, there are many contortionist schools where children are trained in the art of contortion from as young as five years old. Contortionism is also part of the Hindu discipline of yoga.

In the early 20th-century United States, contortionists were popular circus acts. One of the most famous was "Dad" Whitlark, who could still tie his body into pretzel knots and put his face between his ankles at the age of 76. He could also bend over backward and pick up handkerchiefs off the floor with his teeth.

Ethiopian contortionist Kiros Hadgu—alias "The Twisted Kiros"—can dislocate both his arms and his legs and even turn his torso through 180 degrees.

Contortionists are either backbenders or frontbenders, depending on which way their spine is most flexible. A few performers, such as Daniel Browning Smith ("The Rubberboy"), bend both ways (left). He can bend so far backward that the top of his head can touch the seat of his pants and so far forward that he can kiss his own butt!

Frontbending: Frontbenders, like this woman in 1957, twist their body into human knots. In this position they can squeeze through small hoops or tight barrels.

DO KNOT TRY THIS AT HOME

Backbending: As demonstrated by this Mongolian contortionist, backbenders can perform while standing, lying on the floor, or in a headstand position.

Balancing Act: Can you work out which arms and legs belong to whom? A tower of contortionists demonstrate their skills at a show in China.

RIPLEY'S RESEARCH

CONTORTIONISTS ARE OFTEN NATURALLY HIGHLY FLEXIBLE PEOPLE, AND THEY BUILD ON THIS WITH MANY YEARS OF TRAINING. HOWEVER, THE ABILITIES OF MANY CONTORTIONISTS ARE BELIEVED TO BE HEREDITARY. CONTORTIONISTS' VERTEBRAE TEND TO BE SPREAD FARTHER APART THAN A NORMAL SPINE, GIVING THEM EXCEPTIONALLY LONG AND FLEXIBLE LIGAMENTS, WHILE THE COLLAGEN THAT MAKES UP THE LIGAMENTS IS ALSO EXTREMELY SUPPLE. THESE ELEMENTS OF THE SPINE ARE MORE COMMON IN WOMEN, AS FEMALE HORMONES ARE THOUGHT TO HAVE A SOFTENING EFFECT ON COLLAGEN FIBERS. SOME CONTORTIONISTS ARE BORN WITH EHLERS-DANLOS SYNDROME, A CONDITION THAT CAUSES ABNORMAL COLLAGEN PRODUCTION AND CAN THEREFORE INCREASE LIGAMENT ELASTICITY.

Marinelli Bend: Mongolian-born contortionist Iona Luvsandorj can support her entire bodyweight on her mouth in a backbreaking maneuver. She managed to hold the inverted backbend pose, called the Marinelli bend, for 33 seconds in May 2009, her mouth bearing the weight of her body by biting onto a short post.

Split Apart: Ruby Ring, a U.S. contortionist of the 1940s, called herself "The Mother of the Oversplit"—a split of more than 180 degrees. She stood with her legs on two chairs and then, with nothing to hold on to, slid the chairs apart into an eye-watering oversplit.

Man in a Bottle: Argentinian contortionist Hugo Zamoratte specialized in squeezing himself into bottles—but he nearly died while practicing his act in a Santiago, Chile, hotel room in 1982. He became stuck in the bottle, the door of which had accidentally locked, and after 40 minutes in a very uncomfortable position he was starting to hallucinate. He was saved by the timely arrival of a bewildered cleaner, who opened the door of the bottle and freed the exhausted contortionist.

Enterology: Enterologists squeeze themselves into tiny boxes or containers, as demonstrated by this contortionist in 1925.

R HOPPING MAD

An 18th-century maidservant from Godalming, England, became a national sensation when she convinced doctors she had given birth to more than 16 rabbits. In 1726, 25-year-old Mary Toft went into apparent labor overseen by John Howard, a male midwife, who recorded that Mary began producing parts of animals, including nine baby rabbits, in one day! Doctors were fascinated by the births, and explained them as "Maternal Impressions," maintaining that her fantasies about rabbits during her pregnancy had created these defects on the human fetus. Mary later admitted staging the births when it was discovered that a porter had smuggled a rabbit into Mary's chamber. The medical profession of the time suffered a great deal of ridicule as a result.

R 16 TOES

A baby was born with 16 toes—eight on each foot—in Leizhou, Guangdong, China, in November 2008.

R PSALM SAVIOR

An Argentinian pastor survived after a book of psalms he was holding deflected a bullet fired at him at close range. Mauricio Zanes Condori was trying to talk two thieves out of robbing his church in Rodeo del Medio in May 2009 when one of the men fired at his chest from a distance of 7 ft (2 m), but the holy book slowed down the bullet and changed its trajectory.

R RARE TWINS

In a one in a million chance, an American mother gave birth to twins who have different fathers. Mia Washington from Dallas, Texas, gave birth to Justin and Jordan within seven minutes of each other, but in a remarkable twist of fate, they turned out to be half-brothers. Miss Washington admitted having an affair and conceived two babies by different men at the same time.

All Fingers and Toes

The chances of having six healthy fingers on both hands, or six healthy toes on both feet, are very slim, but K.V. Subramaniyan from Kerala Province, India, has both! K.V., an acupuncture doctor who was once punished at school for saying that humans have 12 toes and 12 fingers, has a genetic condition known as polydactyly. Usually this means that someone has an extra finger or toe that is just a piece of tissue, occasionally containing bones without joints, but K.V. has fully functioning extra digits on both of his hands and feet, which is extremely rare.

R MIDAIR DEATH

A novice skydiver landed safely in 2009—even though the instructor to whom he was strapped had died of a heart attack in midair. When they jumped out of a plane above Chester, South Carolina, soldier Daniel Pharr was making his first-ever jump, while 49-year-old instructor George Steele was a veteran of more than 8,000 jumps. However, thousands of feet above the ground as they were finishing their free fall and just moments after their parachute had opened, Steele died. Pharr came down about a third of a mile from the intended drop point despite being able to reach only one of the parachute's steering toggles behind the dead man, forcing him to descend in circles.

R SECRET BABY

Doctors in Qingshen, China, discovered that a 92-year-old woman had been carrying an unborn child in her body for more than 60 years. Huang Yijun, of Huangjiaotan, said her baby had died in her womb in 1948, but she could not afford the money to have the dead fetus removed. Her long-standing secret was finally revealed in 2009 after she hurt her stomach and underwent a hospital scan. Doctors were amazed because normally a dead fetus would decay and cause infection, but Huang had stayed healthy all that time.

R TWIN TOWN

Ten percent of children born in Cândido Godói, Brazil, are twins—and half of them are genetically identical. Twins usually occur in about 1.25 percent of pregnancies.

R SAVED BY DIAPER

Eighteen-month-old Caua Felipe Massaneiro survived a plunge from a third-floor apartment window in Recife, Brazil, in 2008 when his diaper snagged on a security spike, slowing his fall.

Miracle Mother

On the mountains of Rio Talea in southern Mexico, in March 2000, pregnant Inés Ramirez Perez was forced to cut open her own womb to have her baby after suffering for 12 hours with extreme labor pain. With the nearest clinic over 50 mi (80 km) away and no phone to call her husband at the next town, she was completely alone during the procedure. She gulped down rubbing alcohol to numb the pain and then began to cut using a 6-in (15-cm) slaughter knife. She managed to cut away the skin, fat, and muscle before pulling out her baby boy, Orlando Ruiz Ramirez. Inés thinks she operated for about an hour before retrieving her baby and passing out. Her six-year-old son, Benito, returned with help several hours later. Inés is believed to be the only woman to have ever performed a cesarian section on herself.

℞ TWO WOMBS

Seeking a hospital diagnosis for a pain in her abdomen, two-months-pregnant Lindsay Hasaj of London, England, learned that she had two wombs—a one in a million chance.

℞ GRIZZLY ATTACK

In May 2008, Brent Case of Saanich, British Columbia, Canada, managed to drive more than 15 mi (24 km) to find help after a grizzly bear mauled him so badly that he lost part of his scalp. During the attack, he thought that the bear was literally eating his brains.

℞ SOB STORY

For nearly 20 years, Patricia Webster of Kent, England, suffered from crocodile tears syndrome, a rare medical condition that made her cry uncontrollably whenever she ate food. As a side effect of the condition, nerve fibers that should be used for salivation become damaged and regrow into the lacrimal gland, located under the eye, which controls the flow of tears. So when Patricia chewed and swallowed food, she could not keep herself from crying—until her condition was cured using Botox injections.

℞ KEPT ALIVE

At Oxford, England, in January 2009, a baby girl was kept alive in the womb of her dead mother for two days until she could be born safely. Jayne Soliman collapsed from a brain hemorrhage and although she was declared brain dead, doctors kept her heart beating for 48 hours until they had safely delivered baby Aya prematurely at 25 weeks by cesarean section.

SEEING BLUE

In 2007, Shannon Larratt from Canada couldn't resist the chance to have the first ever cosmetic eyeball tattoo. The procedure involved injecting ink into the top layer of his eye with a syringe 40 times, which had the effect of turning the white of Shannon's eye blue. Corneal tattooing is a surgical procedure for patients who have suffered severe eye trauma, but doctors do not recommend having it done for cosmetic reasons.

℞ PREMATURE AGING

Werner Syndrome, a rare genetic disease, causes premature aging—wrinkled skin, baldness, cataracts, and muscular atrophy—by the time a person reaches their early thirties.

℞ MADE HIS POINT

To protest a judge's decision that he must sell part of his farm to settle a debt, Orico Silva of Figueira da Foz, Portugal, chopped off his own finger with a butcher's knife on the court desk.

℞ TRAPPED UNDERGROUND

After the Xinqiao coal mine, in southwestern China's Guizhou Province, was flooded in June 2009, three miners survived for 25 days while they were trapped underground by licking water off the walls.

℞ TODDLER CAUGHT

A group of fairgoers in Port Orange, Florida, caught and saved a toddler who was dropped nearly 40 ft (12 m) from a carnival ride in 2008 as her mother dangled helplessly above the crowd. The mother had become trapped when the ride started up unexpectedly just as she and her little girl were getting off it.

℞ SHIPWRECKED FISHERMEN

After their boat sank in heavy seas off the north coast of Australia in December 2008, two Burmese fishermen survived for almost a month drifting on an ice box in shark-infested waters.

℞ NASTY SHOCK

A Chinese boy survived a 10,000-volt shock in March 2009. He Haoyang had been playing with wires in a field in Sichuan Province when they suddenly broke. He escaped with just burns to his hands because he managed to run a few steps away from the accident site, where the grass was left completely burned.

℞ RAIL BIRTH

A baby girl was born in September 2009 on a high-speed train linking Paris, France, and Brussels, Belgium. The baby was delivered by two doctors and two nurses who were on board and answered a call for assistance while the train was traveling at around 185 mph (300 km/h).

℞ ONE VOICE

British researchers have found a 60-year-old woman who can identify only one voice—that of Scottish actor Sir Sean Connery. She suffers from the rare condition phonagnosia, which leaves her unable to identify anyone speaking on the phone or the radio. She doesn't even recognize her own daughter's voice and resorts to a system of codewords to identify friends and relatives who call.

Bare Face

Swiss artist "Dave" created this portrait of President Obama from multiple painted bodies in unison during a performance in Athens, Greece, in 2009. The use of choreography and paint in this way has been described as a new form of art called "fusionism."

℞ BRAIN REWIRED

Even though she has only half a brain, a ten-year-old German girl has near-perfect vision in one eye. Experts were baffled as to how the girl, who was born missing the right side of her brain (which maps the left field of vision) could have excellent left- and right-field vision in one eye, enabling her to see objects on either side. Scans revealed that her brain had rewired itself before she was born. Retinal nerve fibers carrying visual information from the back of the eye that should have gone to the right hemisphere of the brain diverted to the left instead.

℞ TWINS PEAK

The Indian village of Kodinhi, Kerala, has more than 250 sets of twins born to just 2,000 families—six times the global average.

℞ BLACKOUT RAID

Mark Lester from Norwich, England, was spared jail for robbing a supermarket at gunpoint after a court heard that he suffers from a rare medical condition that makes him have blackouts and causes him to forget his actions. After the robbery he told his mother that he had suffered a nightmare about holding up a store with a gun, but when she recognized him from a TV report, she realized it was more than a bad dream.

℞ MAIL BOY

Four-year-old Jakob Strauss got trapped inside a mailbox in Feldkirch, Austria. He wriggled in after mailmen had left the door open, and managed to close the hatch behind him. After passersby heard his cries for help, firefighters used bolt cutters to free him.

℞ GOLFER BOY

After being struck by lightning while playing golf with friends in Cape Cod, Massachusetts, Michael Utley staggered around with smoke pouring out of his mouth, nose, and ears. His internal tissues were actually boiling and although his heart stopped, he eventually made an almost full recovery.

℞ MEMORABLE BIRTHDAYS

Thirteen months after giving birth to baby Campbell on August 8, 2008 (08/08/08), Alison Miller of Fayetteville, Arkansas, had a second daughter, Molly Reid, on September 9, 2009 (09/09/09).

The Elephant Face Girl

ANITA, BILLED AS "THE ONLY HUMAN ON EARTH WITH A NOSE LIKE AN ELEPHANT'S TRUNK," PERFORMED AT THE CONEY ISLAND SIDESHOW IN NEW YORK, IN 1944. DURING THIS TIME, CONEY ISLAND WAS RENOWNED AS THE WORLD CENTER OF THE AMUSEMENT PARK INDUSTRY.

CONEY ISLAND TRIBUTE

The Barnum & Bailey Greatest Show on Earth

THE GREAT CONEY ISLAND WATER CARNIVAL

AT THE HEIGHT OF ITS POPULARITY IN THE 1920S, A MILLION VISITORS FLOCKED TO CONEY ISLAND EVERY DAY. THEY CAME TO RIDE HUGE ROLLER COASTERS, ENJOY THE THRILLS OF THE BIG WHEEL, AND TO WITNESS AMAZING HUMAN ODDITIES RECRUITED FROM AFRICA, ASIA, AND EUROPE AT THE AMUSEMENT PARK THAT BECAME KNOWN AS "THE PLAYGROUND OF THE WORLD."

Coney Island Today
"Sideshows by the Seashore" continues the Coney Island tradition of showcasing live bizarre and unusual acts.

Formerly an island but now a peninsula, Coney Island is located in southernmost Brooklyn, New York City. Its popularity as a resort grew in the 1860s when the Coney Island and Brooklyn Railroad started to serve the area, and by 1880 it boasted rides and freak shows. For more than fifty years, until World War II, Coney Island was the biggest amusement area in the United States. On just one day in September 1906, no fewer than 200,000 postcards were mailed from Coney Island.

It housed three major amusement parks—Dreamland, Steeplechase Park, and Luna Park. Dreamland was illuminated by one million electric lights, and at night its searchlight beamed 50 mi (80 km) out over the Atlantic Ocean. The brain behind Dreamland was Samuel W. Gumpertz, who scoured the globe in search of human oddities to appear at his sideshows. He made five trips to Asia and five to Africa, bringing back little people, bearded ladies, and more than 3,000 peculiar performers.

In 1904, Gumpertz created Lilliputia, a miniature city inhabited by little people. The "Midget Village" had a population of 300 Lilliputians and was a tremendous success. For extra effect, he even hired a few giants to wander through its streets.

It was during the early 20th century that many of the sideshows were opened, such as The World Circus Freak Show. The ten-in-one sideshows (offering ten acts for a single admission price) offered a steady career for the performers.

Among the stilt walkers who marched around Coney Island advertising the attractions in the early 1920s was a young Englishman named Archie Leach. He would go on to find fame as Hollywood star Cary Grant.

To cater to the influx of visitors, numerous hotels were built, the most outrageous being one in the shape of an elephant. The Elephant Hotel had a cigar store in one front leg while a spiral staircase in a hind leg led visitors up to a shop and the guest rooms. The animal's head, facing the ocean, offered great views through slits where the eyes were located.

When the nearby Brighton Beach Hotel was threatened by sea erosion in 1888, the entire 500-ft-long (150-m), three-story hotel, weighing 6,000 tons, was jacked up on to 120 rail cars and, with the help of six locomotives, was moved inland 600 ft (180 m)—without breaking a single pane of glass!

After World War II interest in the sideshows declined, nearly putting the organizers and performers out of business. Although most of Coney Island's sideshow performers had become extremely wealthy, there was a clear increase in civilized sensibilities and a growing number of people became concerned about exploitation within the shows.

The sideshow hasn't really died out at Coney Island, but the attention has moved away from "freaks" and oddities of the body and now focuses on performers. "Sideshows by the Seashore," founded by Dick Zigun in 1985, offers such exotic attractions as human blockheads, sword swallowers, and fire eaters.

Yet, we can still remember the classic sideshow performers that made Coney Island the sideshow capital of the world…

First Roller Coaster

America's first roller coaster, Switchback Railroad, was opened on Coney Island in 1884. Passengers seated sideways rode a train on undulating tracks over a 600-ft-long (183-m) wooden structure. The train started at a height of 50 ft (15 m) at one end and ran downhill until its momentum ceased. The passengers then got off and attendants pushed the cars over a switch to a higher level. The passengers returned to their seats and rode back to their original point of departure. Admission was five cents and the ride was so popular that designer LaMarcus Thompson made an average of $600 a day. It had cost him just $1,600 to build.

Jean Carroll, The Tattooed Lady

Believe it or not, Jean started in the sideshows as a bearded lady and finished as a tattooed lady. She fell in love with contortionist John Carson but he couldn't bring himself to marry a woman with a beard. So after a 15-year courtship, she removed her beard using electrolysis and then underwent full body tattooing to maintain her sideshow career.

Lionel The Lion-Faced Man

Born in Poland in 1891 as Stephan Bibrowski, Lionel's entire body was covered in long, thick hair. A very intelligent man who spoke five languages, Bibrowski had a variation of hypertrichosis, known as "werewolf disease." He was famous at Coney during the 1920s and performed his gymnastic act at the Dreamland Circus sideshow.

Zip The Pinhead

Born William Henry Johnson in 1842, Zip is thought to have suffered from a condition called microcephaly, leaving him with an oddly tapered head and an ordinary size face. He performed for over 60 years with the Ringling Brothers at Coney Island, billed initially as a "Wild Man," a missing link from Africa. He later became a comic performer, playing the fiddle so badly that people paid him to stop. He died a wealthy man at the age of 84.

Violetta, The Limbless Woman

Born in Germany in 1906, Aloisia Wagner entered the world of show business at the age of 15, acquiring the stage name Violetta. Completely self-sufficient despite being born with no arms or legs, she moved around by hopping. Her sideshow performance involved her singing, but also demonstrated her abilities to sew and to light a cigarette using only her mouth.

Princess Lola The fattest lady at Coney, Princess Lola claimed to weigh 558 lb (253 kg) in August 1949.

Making a Splash

One of the most famous stunts ever to take place at Coney was an attempt to fly a primitive "airplane" from the top of a 50-ft-high (15-m) ride. The plane simply consisted of a wicker basket with muslin-covered wings hinged to the sides. It had no engine, and the wings were operated by the pilot, a local character called Dutch Charley, who pulled a series of cords and pushed pedals. The contraption was duly hauled to the top of the ride and Charley began pedaling furiously. The cord was then cut, freeing the plane, which promptly plunged into the ocean. Charley had to be rescued by lifeguards.

Baby in a Jar

A baby was preserved in formaldehyde at a Coney Island sideshow in 1944. Coney Island has a long history of baby exhibits, courtesy of the Infant Incubator, a show where newborn infants were displayed under the care of a corps of trained nurses. The incubator babies were miraculously saved from the fire that swept through the island in 1911.

The Four Legged Woman

Josephene Myrtle Corbin was billed as the "Four-Legged Woman," as she had the lower limbs of her unformed twin growing from her pelvis. However, these legs were too weak to stand on, and her right leg had a clubbed foot, so she could only use one of her four legs. She went on to have five children after marrying Dr. Clinton Bicknell at the age of 19.

Headless Woman
A performance by an apparently headless woman has been a major attraction at Coney Island sideshows down through the years.

Elephant Execution

The rivalry between the three major parks on Coney Island was fierce. When George Tilyou attracted crowds to Steeplechase Park by beaching an old sailing ship in front of the entrance, the owners of the newly opened Luna Park retaliated by announcing that Topsy, a rogue elephant who had killed three people (including an abusive keeper), would be publicly executed. Opposition from the American Society for the Prevention of Cruelty to Animals ruled out hanging as a method, so it was decided to electrocute her instead. In 1903, an estimated 1,500 people watched as 6,600 volts were sent coursing through the elephant's body, killing her in ten seconds. When Coney Island later burned down, the fire was described as "Topsy's Revenge."

1829 Coney Island House opens

1867 The hot dog is invented at Coney Island!

1876 First carousel built with hand-carved horses and animals, costs five cents a ride

1879 First horse racing track open

1880 New pier means steamships can ferry passengers from Manhattan

1884 Switchback Railroad, America's first roller coaster, is unveiled

1885 Seven-floor Elephant Hotel opens with 31 rooms

1895 16-acre (6.4 ha) Sea Lion Park opens, North America's first enclosed amusement park

1896 The Elephant Hotel burns down

1897 George Tilyou builds Steeplechase Park

1898 Barnum & Bailey open The Great Water Carnival with clowns, amazing swimmers and log rollers

1903 Topsy the killer elephant is executed at Luna Park

1903 Luna Park opens and in just six weeks pays back the $700,000 it cost to build

1904 Dreamland opens, including Lilliputia, a miniature city inhabited by little people

1907 Steeplechase Park, burned down, but it is rebuilt for following season

1911 Huge fire destroys 50 amusement sites, including Dreamland—many animals perish

1917 Fatty Arbuckle and Buster Keaton film the silent comedy movie *Coney Island* at Luna Park

1920 Subway connects Coney Island with Manhattan and Brooklyn

1920 150-ft-tall (46-m) steel Ferris Wonder Wheel opens, holding 144 riders.

1927 Wooden Cyclone roller coaster built, featuring 85-ft (26-m), 60-degree drop

1940 Steeplechase Park buys 250-ft-high (75-m) Parachute Jump ride for $150,000 from New York World's Fair

1947 On July 4, 12,500 people ride the Wonder Wheel

1962 Astroland opens—it closed in 2008.

1964 Steeplechase Park closes

1983 First Coney Island Mermaid Parade held for contestants in marine costumes

1985 "Sideshows by the Seashore" opened as the only "ten-in-one" sideshow (ten acts for one admission price) in North America

1989 Parachute Jump declared a city landmark

2009 "Sideshows by the Seashore" continues to flourish

First Steps Jingle Luis from the Philippines took her first unaided steps at age 15 after doctors at a New York City hospital straightened her severely clubbed feet, which were twisted backward and upside down. Dr. Terry Amaral inserted screws into the bones of her feet and turned the screws bit by bit over a period of six weeks so her feet would rotate, a few degrees at a time, into their correct position.

℞ BAG OF HAIR

Peng Fu, a traveling herbal medicine practitioner from Suining, China, has not cut his hair for over 60 years and carries it around in a bag on his back. When last measured, his hair was 8 ft 10 in (2.7 m) long and weighed nearly 9 lb (4 kg).

℞ TWO-DAY MEMORY

Andy Wray from Essex, England, has a memory that lasts only two days—so if he is parted from his wife or young daughter for 48 hours or more, he can no longer recognize them. He has dissociative amnesia, a condition that effectively wipes his memory clean on a regular basis. Doctors say it is the result of trauma suffered during his time working as a police officer.

℞ ORGANS REVERSED

An Indian man is thought to be the only living person in the world with situs inversus—a condition where his internal organs are back to front. Doctors in Mumbai were about to remove a tumor from the kidney of Ashok Shivnani when they realized that most of his chest and abdominal organs, as well as many blood vessels, were in the mirror opposite position of where they should be in his body.

℞ LOUD SNORER

Jenny Chapman from Cambridgeshire, England, snores more loudly than the noise of a jet aircraft. She snores in her sleep at 111.6 decibels—eight decibels louder than the roar of a low-flying jet. She could drown out the sounds of a spinning washing machine, a diesel truck, or a speeding express train.

℞ EGYPTIAN MUMMY

Mother-of-three Nileen Namita from Brighton, England, has undergone more than 50 cosmetic procedures to make herself look like the ancient Egyptian Queen Nefertiti. Since 1987, Nileen, who believes she is a reincarnation of Nefertiti, has spent over $300,000 on eight nose jobs, three chin implants, one eyebrow lift, three facelifts, six mini facelifts, two lip surgeries, five eye surgeries, and 20 minor facial tweaks—to recreate herself in the image of the "Beauty of the Nile."

℞ MUSCLE BOY

A five-year-old Romanian boy has muscles that are bigger than those of boys over three times his age. Strong boy Giuliano Stroe, who has been training since age two, can perform grueling stunts such as horizontal bar routines, backflips off a table top, and walking on his hands with a weight ball between his legs.

℞ REAL POPEYE

Matthias Schlitte, a German arm wrestler, has a huge right forearm that measures almost 18 in (46 cm) around—over twice the size of his left arm. He is known as the real-life Popeye after the spinach-loving cartoon sailor who has disproportionately muscular forearms.

℞ MIRACLE WALKER

A four-year-old boy who was told by doctors that he would be confined to a wheelchair for the rest of his life has miraculously learned to walk by copying a disabled duckling. Finlay Lomax from Plymouth, England, has cerebral palsy but after his mother took in a day-old duckling with a broken leg, she was amazed to see Finlay standing on his own two feet and mimicking its steps.

℞ TOUGH TEEN

Fifteen-year-old Bobby Natoli of Oswego, New York, did 53 chin-ups in one minute in 2008, surpassing the feat of his father, Robert, who had managed 44 the previous year. Bobby also recorded 209 chin-ups in half an hour when he was just 12 years old.

℞ HAIR SALE

To beat the economic crisis, many women in Spain have started selling their hair. Depending on the length and weight, a ponytail can be worth up to $220 when sold to a company that exports natural hair for wigs and extensions.

℞ CHOPSTICK IMPALEMENT

Doctors in China removed a chopstick that was lodged 0.15 in (4 mm) into the brain of a 14-month-old boy. Li Jingchao, from Shandong Province, was playing with chopsticks when he fell on one and it went up his nose and into his brain.

℞ FLU SHOTS

The University of Central Florida administered 2,527 flu shots to staff, students, and local residents in eight hours in September 2009.

℞ SIMPSONS SAVIOR

Choking to death on a sandwich, ten-year-old Alex Hardy from Wakefield, England, was saved by his best friend Aiden Bateman who performed an abdominal thrust maneuver— remembering the technique from an episode of *The Simpsons*.

℞ STRANGER'S DIAGNOSIS

A stranger saved the life of a Spanish bus passenger by telling her that she might be suffering from a rare disease. Montse Ventura was on a bus in Barcelona in 2009, when a woman sitting opposite noticed her unusually shaped hands. She urged Montse to have tests for acromegaly, a disorder caused by a pituitary gland problems that causes abnormal growth of hands and feet. Sure enough, when Montse went to the doctor, a small pituitary gland tumor was found and removed.

℞ VIOLENT SNEEZE

Victoria Kenny from Chichester, England, broke her back—just by sneezing. She sneezed with such force that she ruptured a disk in her spine, leaving her paralyzed for almost two years.

Blood Portrait

A $450,000 self-portrait sculpted by British artist Marc Quinn from his own frozen blood was put on display at London's National Portrait Gallery in 2009. Quinn made his first blood head in 1991, and has subsequently produced a new cast every few years to illustrate how he has aged. He uses 10 pt (4.7 l) of blood for each work, the blood being removed by his doctor, a pint at a time every six weeks.

ICE ORDEAL

Latvian illusionist Gennady Palychevsky was on the verge of literally freezing to death after spending more than 64 hours as a human ice cube. He survived for nearly three days in the 6-sq-ft (0.5-sq-m) ice cube in Moscow before signaling for help because he was suffering from severe frostbite. Palychevsky, who had trained in ice baths for six months, did not eat or drink while sealed inside his ice tomb.

Gallery

IF YOU WOULD LIKE TO FIND OUT MORE ABOUT THESE ODD WAX CREATIONS, CHECK OUT PAGES 8–9.

SARA DISK WEARER OF AFRICA
The Ubangi women of the Sara tribe in Chad, Africa, wear wooden plates in their lips to make them unattractive to raiders.

CROCODILE MAN
Bobby Blackburn from South Africa wears crocodile-teeth dentures, sharp enough to cut through the thickest of meats.

SHOWCASING SOME OF THE MOST BIZARRE AND WEIRD FOLK THAT ROBERT RIPLEY FOUND ON HIS TRAVELS, A VAST MODERN COLLECTION OF WAX HEADS ARE CENTRAL TO THE WORLD OF RIPLEY'S. LOCATED IN RIPLEY MUSEUMS ALL OVER THE WORLD, THE HEADS ARE MADE BY A DEDICATED TEAM OF SCULPTORS, MAKEUP EXPERTS, COSTUME DESIGNERS, AND HAIR SPECIALISTS. THE TEAM SPENDS ITS DAYS SURROUNDED BY EXTRAORDINARY ODDITIES IN THE RIPLEY'S ART DEPARTMENT IN FLORIDA. THEY MAKE THE EERILY LIFELIKE HEADS BY PAINSTAKINGLY STICKING EACH STRAND OF HAIR TO THE SCULPTURES AND PAINTING EACH INDIVIDUAL WRINKLE, BELIEVE IT OR NOT!

HUMAN UNICORN
A man named Weng, found by Ripley in Manchuria, China, in 1931, had a 13-in (33-cm) horn growing out of the back of his head.

MAN WITH THE GOLDEN NOSE
Sixteenth-century Danish astronomer Tycho Brahe lost his nose in a sword fight and replaced it with a solid gold replica.

WOLF MAN
Based on the 1931 Lon Chaney movie *The Wolf Man*, Larry Talbot is bitten by a wolf and gradually and horrifyingly becomes one.

JO-JO THE DOG-FACED MAN
Born in Russia, Fedor Jeftichew suffered from hypertrichosis, or "Werewolf syndrome," and his body was covered with hair up to 8 in (20 cm) long. He was known as Jo-Jo the Dog-faced Man when he became a famous sideshow performer.

EYE-POPPER
Avelino Perez Matos from Baracoa, Cuba, could dislocate his eyes from their sockets whenever he wanted.

LONGEST NOSE IN HISTORY
Thomas Wedders, an 18th-century sideshow entertainer from England, had a nose that measured an incredible 7½ in (19 cm) long.

RIPLEY'S HEROES

LIGHTHOUSE MAN
Using a 7-in (18-cm) lighted candle inserted in his head, the Lighthouse Man would act as a human lantern in the unlit alleys of Chunking, China, in the 1930s. He had cut a hole through the bone in his scalp so the candle could be held in place with sealing wax.

GRACE McDANIELS
Billed as the "mule faced woman" during her successful sideshow career, when Grace revealed her face at sideshows, men and women would sometimes faint.

PADAUNG WOMAN OF MYANMAR
The women of the Padaung tribe add a gold ring around their neck annually, to a maximum of 20 rings, which can make their neck 15 in (38 cm) long.

R WAR WOUND

More than 60 years after being wounded by a mortar shell in World War II, John Ready of London, England, still had pieces of shrapnel working their way out of his skin.

R TOTALLY TATTOOED

Since having his first tattoo of a small juggling club on his hip, Australian entertainer Lucky Diamond Rich has had 100 percent of his body tattooed. He even has tattoos on top of tattoos!

R KNUCKLE CRACK

The sound caused by a person cracking their knuckles comes from gas bubbles forming and collapsing with a snapping noise.

R POWERFUL PERFUME

Thirty-four people were hospitalized in Texas in July 2009—by strong perfume. Employees at a Bank of America call center in Fort Worth felt dizzy, nauseous, and short of breath after a coworker sprayed perfume. As panic spread through the building, workers poured on to the sidewalk outside and another 110 people were treated at the scene for chest pains and headaches.

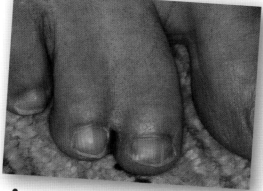

Webbed Wonder

Although normal in birds, reptiles, amphibians, and some mammals, syndactyly—or webbed toes—is a rare condition in humans, occurring in about one in 2,500 births. Usually the second and third toes are joined by skin and flexible tissue. The cause in humans is unknown, but it is sometimes hereditary. Famous people with webbed toes include actors Dan Aykroyd and Ashton Kutcher, and former Soviet leader Joseph Stalin.

R BABY ALLERGY

Having suffered several blisters and a burning rash after giving birth, Joanne Mackie of Birmingham, England, discovered she was allergic to her own baby. A rare skin disease, *Pemphigoid gestationis*, that developed while she was still pregnant meant that she could not even cuddle baby James or pick him up for the first month of his life because the blisters caused her such pain. To feed him from a bottle, she had to wrap damp towels around her arms.

R LUCKY GIFT

Schoolgirl Sophie Frost of Rayleigh, Essex, England, owes her life to the iPod she was wearing when struck by lightning. She survived the 30,000-volt surge only because it traveled through the gadget's wire, diverting it away from her vital organs. She had been given the iPod just four days earlier as a gift from her grandmother.

Folds of Skin

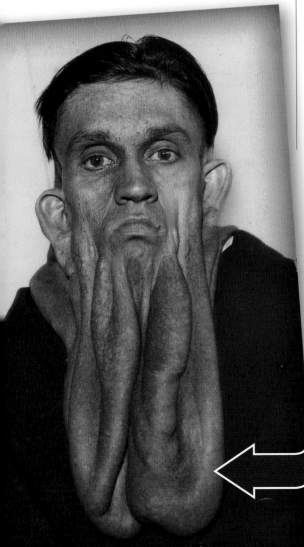

Arthur Loos, who performed at the Ripley Odditorium in Chicago in 1933, had huge folds of skin hanging down from his face. He suffered from neurofibromatosis, which causes extreme skin abnormalities.

R SLEEP PLUNGE

Marius Purcariu from Arad, Romania, escaped with only minor injuries after falling from a fourth-floor window while he was asleep. He was found wrapped in a curtain on the hood of a car parked beneath his bedroom window. Doctors said that because he was sleepwalking his body was relaxed during the fall, which probably saved his life.

R SEVERED EAR

Doctors in Cologne, Germany, saved a woman's severed ear by stitching it to her buttocks. Julia Schwarz's right ear was bitten off in a fight, but the surgeons' first attempt to sew it back failed because the side of her head had not healed sufficiently. While waiting to carry out a second operation, they made a small incision in her butt and stitched the severed lobe into the pocket, keeping it there until her head had healed.

R LAUGHTER LESSONS

After a study revealed that Germans laugh on average for just six minutes a day, an organization of yoga-laughter therapists was set up in Cologne to teach Germans how to laugh. Laughter is considered healthy and the perfect antidote to aging. There are more than 6,000 laughter clubs around the world on five continents and there is even an annual World Laughter Day.

R STRETCH BRIDE

Suffering from a rare kind of dwarfism, Tiffanie DiDonato of Jacksonville, North Carolina, underwent bone-lengthening procedures so that her body could be stretched an incredible 14 in (35 cm), from 3 ft 8 in to 4 ft 10 in (1.14 m to 1.45 m), in time for her wedding day. Surgeons broke her bones and then inserted a device that slowly pulls them apart. The bone then grows and fills in the gaps so that each day her legs would be stretched another 0.04 in (1 mm). Diastrophic dysplasia (dwarfism) had caused Tiffanie to stop growing at age eight.

R HUMAN LIGHT

Our bodies emit tiny amounts of light a thousand times weaker than the human eye can perceive. The light levels are at their highest in late afternoon and at their lowest late at night, and the brightest light is emitted from the cheeks, forehead, and neck. It is the result of bioluminescence, a side effect of metabolic reactions within all creatures.

SHARP FEATURES

Retired bank manager John Lynch of Hertfordshire, England, has over 240 body piercings. He has more than 150 on his head and neck alone and has had to give up flying because he kept setting off airport security scanners. He also has hundreds of tattoos, including an image of Marilyn Monroe that covers most of his torso. He did not get his first piercing until he was in his forties.

THE CORAL MEN

Lin Tianzhuan from Shuimen, southern China, first noticed the growths on his hands and feet when he was 13, and over the next 25 years they gradually spread and hardened to the point where he could no longer bend his arms or legs. Dubbed "Coral Boy" by friends and neighbors, Lin became a hermit, hiding himself away at the family home. "If I had to go out I wrapped myself up in blankets because people would scream when they saw me."

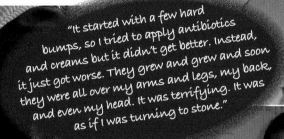

"It started with a few hard bumps, so I tried to apply antibiotics and creams but it didn't get better. Instead, it just got worse. They grew and grew and soon were all over my arms and legs, my back, and even my head. It was terrifying. It was as if I was turning to stone."

Now, after a year of treatment and surgery at a specialist skin clinic, the dark brown shells have been cut away and he has nothing worse than a few discolored skin patches to remind him of his previous horrific condition.

 BEFORE

 AFTER

RIPLEY'S RESEARCH

THE CONDITION IS THOUGHT TO BE CAUSED BY THE HUMAN PAPILLOMA VIRUS, A FAIRLY COMMON INFECTION, WHICH USUALLY CAUSES ONLY SMALL WARTS. HOWEVER, IF THE PATIENT SUFFERS FROM A PARTICULAR IMMUNE-SYSTEM DEFICIENCY, THE BODY IS UNABLE TO CONTAIN THE WARTS AND ALLOWS THE VIRUS TO SPREAD AND PRODUCE EXTREME GROWTHS KNOWN AS "CUTANEOUS HORNS." FEWER THAN 200 PEOPLE WORLDWIDE ARE THOUGHT TO SUFFER FROM THIS MYSTERIOUS IMMUNE PROBLEM.

The Root of the Problem

Lin's case is similar to that of Dede Koswara, the Indonesian "tree man." After cutting his knee as a teenager, a small wart developed on his leg and spread uncontrollably so that most of his body was encased in strange treelike growths. The only work he could find was as a sideshow performer and so, when offered the chance of a cure, he was initially reluctant to take it because he would lose his livelihood. Eventually, Dede reconsidered and has undergone nine operations to remove more than 17 lb (8 kg) of gnarled warts from his body.

Geoff has a coat of arms tattooed on his right foot.

Close-up of bird-of-paradise flowers on Geoff's right thigh.

Sunflowers are depicted in intricate detail on his left thigh.

This elaborate red flower is tattooed on the back of one of Geoff's knees.

Still Live

Retired history teacher Geoff Ostling from Sydney, Australia, is literally a walking work of art. More than 20 years ago, Geoff began working with well-known tattoo artist eX de Merci, choosing the theme of Australian flowers, and they now cover his skin from neck to toe, depicting every flower he could think of. When Geoff dies, he wants to be skinned and the tattoos displayed whole, just as they are on his body, at Australia's National Gallery in Canberra. He has already lined up the help of a taxidermist for when that day comes.

ℛ SINKHOLE HELL

Jeanne Schnepp, 63, spent nearly a week stuck on a raft in a sinkhole on the Wapsipinicon River in Iowa. She had been fishing from the rubber raft when the strong river current swept her downstream and deposited her in the sinkhole, trapping her between a 12-ft (3.6-m) wall of rocks and a logjam she couldn't climb over. After enduring two thunderstorms, hot days, and cold nights, she was finally spotted by an angler.

ℛ TATTOO NERD

Computer nerds have been getting their bodies tattooed with images relating to their laptops. Among popular tattoo requests are a USB cable, the Apple logo, and various items of software.

ℛ SHRAPNEL DISLODGED

A piece of shrapnel that had been lodged in the jaw of Alf Mann from Birmingham, England, for 65 years suddenly dropped out in 2009. Alf had struggled to speak and eat properly since being injured by an explosion during World War II—but one morning he woke to find blood on his pillow, along with the $1/2$-in (1.2-cm) piece of shrapnel.

ℛ JEEP ADVENTURE

A three-year-old boy was rescued in July 2009 after riding his toy jeep into the Peace River, British Columbia, Canada, and floating nearly 8 mi (13 km) downstream. He was found still sitting happily in his battery-powered jeep in water that was 15 ft (4.5 m) deep.

ℛ MAGIC TOOTH

After being blind for 12 years following an accident at work, Martin Jones from Yorkshire, England, had his sight restored in 2009 by having a tooth transplanted into his eye. One of his canine teeth was removed and converted into a holder for a special optical lens by drilling a hole in it. Then the tooth was inserted into his cheek for three months to enable it to grow new tissue and blood vessels. The tooth was then fitted with the lens and inserted into his right eyeball. Two weeks later, his sight returned and for the first time he was able to see his wife Gill, whom he had married in 2005.

ℛ BROKE FALL

A six-year-old boy survived a 70-ft (21-m) fall from an apartment balcony in Gothenburg, Sweden, in September 2009 when a passerby, who had stopped when he saw the boy fall, managed to catch him.

ℛ TWO WOMBS

Sarah Reinfelder of Sault Ste. Marie, Michigan, who has two wombs, gave birth to twin daughters in February 2009—one from each uterus.

ℛ BODY STRENGTH

At age 83, Sidney Williams of Port Elizabeth, South Africa, can lift up to 353 lb (160 kg) even though he himself weighs only 220 lb (100 kg)—that means he can lift 50 percent more than his body weight.

Needlework

Anatomical technician and embalmer W. K. Foster from Winnipeg, Canada, collected more than 30 tattoos that he removed from dead bodies at the medical college where he worked in the 1920s. Robert Ripley dubbed it the "World's Strangest Art Collection" and displayed a selection at the first Ripley Odditorium in Chicago in 1933. The display is now at the Ripley's museum in St. Augustine, Florida.

Big Deal

A German art collector paid $215,000 to buy this vibrant tattoo of the Virgin Mary—even though it was tattooed on somebody else's back. The work, by Belgian artist Wim Delvoye, is on the back of Tim Steiner from Switzerland, who is now an exhibit himself. Steiner has to show the piece three times a year, and is also bound by an agreement that means the tattooed skin will be returned to its new owner after his death.

It's not the first time prized tattoos by Wim Delvoye have been for sale. A French man tried to give a Paris museum his tattoo in his will, and a British man attempted to sell his own piece of skin art in an auction—both have failed to find a buyer so far.

ACKNOWLEDGMENTS

COVER (b) Photographer: Sridar Sri; 6–7 Simon De Trey-White/Barcroft Media Ltd; 8 (t/l) Beretta/Sims/Rex Features; 9 Kevin Smith/Solent News/Rex Features; 10 Miami New Times/Colby Katz; 11 (l) © EuroPics[CEN]; 12 (b/r) © Andy Rain/EPA/Corbis, (b/l) Archive Holdings Inc./Hulton Archive/Getty Images, (t/r) Geoffrey Swaine/Rex Features, (t/l) Wierzblicki/BEI/Rex Features; 13 (t/l) Wenn.com, (b/r) Rex Features, (b/l) FPG/Staff/Hulton Archive /Getty Images, (t/r) ©Sky1/Andi Southam; 14 Photographer: Sridar Sri; 15 (t/l, t/r) Jaime Puebla/AP/Press Association Images, (b) Lane Jensen/BizarreArchive.com; 16 Reuters/Yiorgos Karahalis; 17 Eileen Darby/Time Life Pictures/Getty Images; 18 Courtesy Everett Collection/Rex Features; 19 Getty Images; 20 (t/l, b, t/r) D. B. Denholtz Collection; 21 (b) Time & Life Pictures/Getty Images, (b/l) D. B. Denholtz Collection; 22 (t/l) Time & Life Pictures/Getty Images, (t) D. B. Denholtz Collection; 24 Richard Drew/AP/Press Association Images; 25 (t/r) Dazed & Confused/Rex Features, (b) © EuroPics[CEN]; 28 (t) © NHPA/Photoshot; 29 Rex Features; 30 © EuroPics[CEN]; 31 Reuters/Supri Supri; 32 (t/l) James Elsby/Newspix/Rex Features; 33 Picture courtesy de Pury & Luxembourg, Switzerland & Studio Wim Delvoye, Belgium

Key: t = top, b = bottom, c = center, l = left, r = right, sp = single page, dp = double page

All other photos are from Ripley Entertainment Inc.
Every attempt has been made to acknowledge correctly and contact copyright holders and we apologize in advance
for any unintentional errors or omissions, which will be corrected in future editions.

DISCARD

ACKNOWLEDGMENTS

COVER (b) Photographer: Sridar Sri; 6–7 Simon De Trey-White/Barcroft Media Ltd; 8 (t/l) Beretta/Sims/Rex Features; 9 Kevin Smith/Solent News/Rex Features; 10 Miami New Times/Colby Katz; 11 (l) © EuroPics[CEN]; 12 (b/r) © Andy Rain/EPA/Corbis, (b/l) Archive Holdings Inc./Hulton Archive/Getty Images, (t/r) Geoffrey Swaine/Rex Features, (t/l) Wierzblicki/BEI/Rex Features; 13 (t/l) Wenn.com, (b/r) Rex Features, (b/l) FPG/Staff/Hulton Archive /Getty Images, (t/r) ©Sky1/Andi Southam; 14 Photographer: Sridar Sri; 15 (t/l, t/r) Jaime Puebla/AP/Press Association Images, (b) Lane Jensen/BizarreArchive.com; 16 Reuters/Yiorgos Karahalis; 17 Eileen Darby/Time Life Pictures/Getty Images; 18 Courtesy Everett Collection/Rex Features; 19 Getty Images; 20 (t/l, b, t/r) D. B. Denholtz Collection; 21 (b) Time & Life Pictures/Getty Images, (b/l) D. B. Denholtz Collection; 22 (t/l) Time & Life Pictures/Getty Images, (t) D. B. Denholtz Collection; 24 Richard Drew/AP/Press Association Images; 25 (t/r) Dazed & Confused/Rex Features, (b) © EuroPics[CEN]; 28 (t) © NHPA/Photoshot; 29 Rex Features; 30 © EuroPics[CEN]; 31 Reuters/Supri Supri; 32 (t/l) James Elsby/Newspix/Rex Features; 33 Picture courtesy de Pury & Luxembourg, Switzerland & Studio Wim Delvoye, Belgium

Key: t = top, b = bottom, c = center, l = left, r = right, sp = single page, dp = double page

All other photos are from Ripley Entertainment Inc.
Every attempt has been made to acknowledge correctly and contact copyright holders and we apologize in advance for any unintentional errors or omissions, which will be corrected in future editions.